Poems for a Cartoon Mouse

Andrew Burt

Ben Yehuda Press
Teaneck, New Jersey

POEMS FOR A CARTOON MOUSE ©2023 Andrew Burt. All rights reserved. No part of this book may be used or reproduced in any manner whatsoever without written permission except in the case of brief quotations embodied in critical articles and reviews.

Published by Ben Yehuda Press
122 Ayers Court #1B
Teaneck, NJ 07666

http://www.BenYehudaPress.com

To subscribe to our monthly book club and support independent Jewish publishing, visit https://www.patreon.com/BenYehudaPress

Jewish Poetry Project #33   http://jpoetry.us

Ben Yehuda Press books may be purchased at a discount by synagogues, book clubs, and other institutions buying in bulk. For information, please email markets@BenYehudaPress.com

Cover art by Sandra C. Burt.

ISBN13 978-1-953829-53-5

23 24 25 / 10 9 8 7 6 5 4 3 2 1   20231024

Also by Andrew Burt:

American Hysteria

For Claudia

Contents

Departing Shostka, Russia	2
The Ship	3
Passing By A Weeping Willow On The Riverbank	4
Ellis Island Pigeons	5
Immigrant Mouse Arrives In New York, Circa 1900	6
Instructions For What To Do Upon Losing Your Family	8
Song Of A Cat Who Terrorizes The Neighborhood	9
Old Clock	10
Fievel's Ode	12
Mouse As Mask	13
Homesickness	14
Instructions For What To Do Upon Losing Your Family	15
Mouse Thinks About The Meaning Of Manifest Destiny While Also Channeling Walt Whitman In A Poem About New York	16
Certificate Of Naturalization	18
Street Fight	19
Mouse Gets Picked On	20
Instructions For What To Do Upon Losing Your Family	21
Traveler's Prayer While Stranded In A Snowstorm	22
Walking Down A Vegetable Aisle In A Farmer's Market	23
Mouse Goes Spelunking At Summer Camp	24
Mouse Wants To Go Shopping On Moving Day But Really It's Just The Hormones	25
5 Instructions On How To Lose Your Family	26
Cape Cutty	27
Father Mouse Plays Violin Late At Night On The Roof	28
Mouse And The Cowboys	29
Poem For Andrew Jackson	30
On Comparing Post-Sleep Disorientation (Also Known As "Confusional Arousal") To Fievel Discovering America And Being Surprised By What He Sees	31
On Thinking About Nazism, Walt Disney Late At Night	32
Mouse Discovers The Existence Of Evil	33
Advice For A Teenage Mouse	34
Mouse Tries To Feel Good About The Future	35
Before Dawn	36

Poem About A Lost Hat	37
Mouse's Prayer	38
Mouse Doubts Poetry's Utility	39
Instructions For What To Do Upon Losing Your Family	40
Haircut	41
Bath	42
Mouse Makes Love	43
Mouse Breaks Up With Girlfriend	44
Father Mouse Loses His Temper And Yells At A 3-Year-Old During A Birthday Party	45
Father Mouse Apologizes By Attempting To Explain The Meaning Of Life	46
Advice For A Grown-Up Mouse	47
Dialogue Between Father and Son, In Two Parts	48
Four Endings For A Cartoon Mouse	49
Author's Note	51
About the Author	53

We'll ride the roaring rivers
Turn wilderness into towns
Our dreams will take us up and up
And never let us down.

—Educated Mouse, from *Fievel Goes West*

"There's no climax . . . no clear beginning, middle or end."

—The Austin City Chronicle on *Fievel Goes West*

Departing Shostka, Russia

It would be foolish to leave in this
Storm, where one can't even see where
One is going—but I will.

Take Lot
Walking. Take Lot walking with his
Back turned to the world, and his eyes
Forward.

Now, take
The snow moving down to earth, and
The silence as it falls, slowly,
For falling's sake.

The Ship

Here on this boat
Darkness settles:
Ten thousand immigrants
Stand on swollen legs
Their hopes like wooden
Puzzle pieces stacked
To fall: each one built atop
The other: as if distinct:
When really not at all.

Passing By A Weeping Willow On The Riverbank

I.

There is grace to your failure,
Or perhaps it is simply your pride:
Your leaves like clumps of
Pulled hair, pitted against gravity's tug.

II.

You will be forgotten. But so too
Will your forgetters and the rain
Will come down as it comes down
Now: illuminating the water and
The grass in a temporary wet film.

III.

Therefore: sleep, and tower above
The river as it passes, and wilt,
And sway, and do not let the wind
Unhinge whatever it is you believe
Your hands refuse to let go.

Ellis Island Pigeons

Call it a disease
Your flying:
Each moment
Is a movement
Forward, a nose-
Dive out of the
Past. I think of
Movere, like the
Third person,
Singular form
Of trading one
Place for one
Other. Or of
Momentum, as
In moving for
Moving's sake.
Therefore, hold
Me tight and
Let the endless
August nights
Pass. Allow me
The unrelenting
Smoothness of
Your skin. And
Above all do
Not let me fly.
Stand me still
So that I never
Trade one mo-
Ment for the
Next, just for
Moving's sake.

Immigrant Mouse Arrives In New York, Circa 1900

After Lorca

Between the East River and the Bronx
Boys sink through bricks, hammers, soot and steel.
Two hundred thousand of them rip money out of rocks
While a few trace cursive into notebooks—

The lucky ones
Who sleep when they are tired,
Like the river and the leaves
Tumbling in place as the night comes.

But most boys fight with industry
Far into the night
Their thick accents and muffled smoking.
They do not look at the clouds
Or gaze at the ferns
Or hear the steel drums playing.

By morning the moon leaves on its pulley
The rains return to pierce the sky
And the caskets take back the tired
Who stopped working.

New York of silt
New York of wires and death
What hides in your muscles?
What is gained that is not lost
In your relentless working?

*

Tomorrow is made of rocks and time;
Is the draft that sweeps sleepily
Through the fallen branches.
Men watch their dreams decompose on plywood
Shelves like so many cans of rotting corn
And the boys are there to stack
And to restack the shelves again.

But all is not lost: an immigrant
Can, if he wants, find his desires in the grains
Of nakedness or the spit of steel
Or the family that awaits him,
Hauling fruit through sickened streets.

The sky is filled with beaches
For those too timid to take their wants
No matter how unwelcome they be.
It is never agony to forget.
And you have made it this far.

*

So here is my advice: long for cunts
Or cocks or whisky marinate on melting ice
And sweat through days of cigarette
Smoke so dense you cannot enjoy it
And when you sleep, sleep
So that nothing but the cleft
Of your shoes on the sawdusted floors
Of the factories remains.
Let the thick air of the darkening
Night strip the flowers bare
While a child black with soot announces
The Kingdom of Grain is finally here.

Instructions For What To Do Upon Losing Your Family

Prayer

Call yourself lucky. You are alive and fifteen thousand blades of grass bend under the wind in the city park beside you. Some reflect the beams of the rising sun. Think: your mother did not die in childbirth. Nor did your immigrant ship sink on the elbows of the Atlantic as the gray clouds swiped at its mast. Forget your hunger and call this perspective. Find something to thank. Call each gratefulness a prayer.

Song Of A Cat Who Terrorizes The Neighborhood

If morning is forgiveness let it
Stay dark—streetlights slap at the
Shadows, bouncing off the walks
And I am hungry, and unclothed.

None of this was meant to be:
The trashcans gleaming upright,
The mice wooded up their holes,
Echoes that reverberate the night,

And me, idling, forgot. All must go
For them to see—this neighborhood,
These houses and the walls they keep—
Will stand for nothing, if not for me.

Old Clock

For Jean Foreman
In memory of Philip Amsterdam

In an abandoned library　　　　In 1936
A fruitseller takes a wrench
To a clock　　　No bigger
Than a milkcrate
He cannot afford.
So, at least, goes the first part
Of that story:　Old pendulum
Of east　　　　And west
Clock laborer　　　　With tired hands
Whose great-grandchildren　Will become
Rich　　As if in validation.

Here is the second part:
That you grew　　　　Old under
The weight　　　Of your movement
That the sounds　　　Of the dockyard
Kept your sons awake　　　　And your wife
Would die before returning　　　　To Russia.

Now the sun sets　　　On the crumbling
Front stoop　　　You erected
As if in memoriam　　　And your children
Decompose　　　On balconies
Like the Yiddish　　　You refused to teach
Their framed glasses　　　　Reflecting the warmth
Of the setting　　　Florida sun.
And what is left　　If not
The sounds　　　Made by the things
That have long ago　　　Stopped working?

Old clock,
Prove to me   That life is more
Than a back   And forth
Separated   By a silence
That is endless   And is unintended.

Fievel's Ode

This country is like a marshmallow
Fire at summer camp. Here is

What they say: When you are
Rich you roast your food to

Burning just for fun. You take
Chocolate and melt it. You grab

What you want from the market
And there is no fighting over

Food. Somewhere a violin moans
Because it is hungry. But how

Could it not but be fed
If what they say is true:

That America is where dreams find
Hope before finding you.

Mouse As Mask

Mouse is not new, but neither
Is mask: the objects we use
As walls to close our eyes
Behind.

Think: *Tom and Jerry, Maus,
Bugs Bunny,* even *Pinky
And the Brain.*

But think also of a Pirandello play
Where every character is honest
Because that is what masks do:

Like a screen dangling safely
Before a broken windowpane,
Used for whatever you want it to.

Homesickness

Will go away as traffic's honking
Is diluted into air

No matter where it came from,
Or what it took to get there.

Instructions For What To Do Upon Losing Your Family

Stealing

If you are hungry
Set your hunger free.

Rules and morals
Exist to be broken

Or else followed,
Unknowingly.

Mouse Thinks About The Meaning Of Manifest Destiny While Also Channeling Walt Whitman In A Poem About New York

I'll die like everyone else here
        On a dusted wooden floor
Of the apartment we were all
Born into,
Spread-eagle below an unmoved fan.

Here:
Where the buildings pay forgotten
Tributes to forgotten ceilings
Of the sky.

Outside, there is nothing the sky has not
Abandoned
        But the tilled cement
And the swirling pigeons
Who pick at anything,
Fruitlessly,
        Like nothing wasn't theirs.

It is empty here,
In the canyon-shifts below the skyline,
And between the floating crusts
        Of bodies that sidewalk these streets
A solitary hope drifts like a leaf
Skating in the wind.

That hope is me.

I am the hope that has not been forgotten
Because I declare myself welcome
        Here,
As if there is nothing in history
I will not make mine. As if there is nowhere

      I will not claim
Because my feet tread flags
And each footstep is my own.

Here:
      The unmoving brick,
The unmoved heavens,
Nobody's home.

Certificate Of Naturalization

BE IT REMEMBERED
that you are not the only one HAVING APPLIED
TO BE ADMITTED having forgotten
the piles of grain you left your six sisters
to tend to back home—

                a word that
in 1906 I'd imagine SAID PETITIONER
INTENDS TO RESIDE PERMANENTLY
having made a choice that has only
just begun.

I would also imagine beginnings
like these an opportunity to burn AT LEAST
ONE YEAR PRECEEDING the day you left
a circle of women huddled to see you go
the spring still cold, the dew not yet formed
and all the promises you made to write and send
money and perhaps even to telegraph
left skating, over time, like spent matches
in rained-in potholes.

BE IT REMEMBERED that new lives come
on top of old ones, if at all.

Street Fight

Outside on the concrete
Two men shift and duck,
Their fists balled, slicing
The air. One woman nearby
Is shouting: *Fuck 'em up,
Bobby!* But the truth is
This brawl is one of ten
Thousand tonight and
No one cares—police
Will come and end this
Fight, sending home
The small crowd just
Beginning to gather
Around the two men,
Sweaty now and grunting,
As they do what they must
To get recognized.

Mouse Gets Picked On

When I was eleven
Three boys jumped
Out of a bathroom
Stall at summer camp
And fit a trash can
Around my torso.
I could not breathe
But I was safe for as
Long as I was inside.

Instructions For What To Do Upon Losing Your Family

Write A Will

Nothing is as bad as it sounds,
As in the marmalade ice cream
You puckered after tasting that
I ate all of, or the Schoenberg waltz

That sounds like noise even still—
Or the flight we missed in Miami
And spent the night dragging
Our cases throughout the darkened

Airport; where we stood for hours
Watching planes push back against
The earth, taking off, one by one,

Their defiant rumble, and then
Watched as others acquiesced, as if
Falling, and were pulled gently home.

Traveler's Prayer While Stranded In A Snowstorm

Stranded in Chicago O'Hare, let it be home
That I reach—eventually—by way of all

These planes, whose bellies sag like stuffed
Mice, sliding in and out the gates. Once,

In Hebrew school, I asked how we know
That Abraham did not kill Isaac—the angel did

Not come too late and, discovering the body, turn
Into the son. The rabbi told me we shouldn't care

As Abraham surely would not either
If, creating a vacuum, God gave him air.

Walking Down A Vegetable Aisle In A Farmer's Market

In the vegetable aisle a carrot rests
Atop a crate of browning
Asparagus,
Like a solitary line in a stanza
Resenting its loneliness.

Which make one think:
Why even try to sort the artichokes
From the bell peppers if all that
Work can so easily be undone?

Is it that there is order in the green
And blue wood separating the crates?
And imagine life without it:
Chaos in the aisles of the market!
Business most certainly does not like
That sort of thing…

But neither
Does it like poetry and writing
Covers each item already, in stickers
And charts, detailing origins and
Tallying carbs. No, so far as I can tell
All these vegetables are binned
Because it is easier on the eyes.
Therefore, let us go on as always
Dividing ourselves into tribes.

Mouse Goes Spelunking At Summer Camp

It is dark inside this cave
Without your parents.
Thank God for this:
Heavy stick of light
Whose beams emanate
At first close together
But then spread apart.

**Mouse Wants To Go Shopping On Moving Day
But Really It's Just The Hormones**

The trick is that it is empty
Inside, as when you bent over
To put the newspaper-wrapped
Mugs as a bottom layer for
The bubble-wrapped plates. Or
How the girls all hide their warm
Vaginas quietly inside shopping
Malls, shuffling after clothes
They do not need.
Here anything fits:
As in the allure of beginning
Empty, but ending filled.

5 Instructions On How To Lose Your Family

1. Breathe.
2. Travel to America.
3. Or not.
4. It's just as well to sleep and forget.
5. And then to go about your days.

Cape Cutty

Jut-stream bends beyond the horizon. Ten thousand poets died here, looking for something new. Was it vanity, chaos they were after? Was it poetry or prose? What unwritten words last fell from their lips?

*

O what laziness in discovery! How singular Jackson Pollock or Cortez! And yet what sacrifice!

*

Somewhere in the far north it is night. A glacier melts beneath winter's shadow. A hand extends casually from the unforgiving snow.

Father Mouse Plays Violin Late At Night On The Roof

Midnight is when the violin
Moans its loudest: in soft
Hues while the others sleep.

Father climbs the fire escape,
Arcs his neck around the
Instrument's chin. Once,

I climbed through the window
And watched him walk two
Stories up, slouch, then play.

His shadow sliding from the
Streetlight across the bricks
Of our building. How his feet

Shook the grated staircase.
How for once he let himself
Waver where he stood.

Mouse And The Cowboys

*"Lincoln may have made men free,
But Sam Colt made them equal."*

   —Frontier saying from the late 1800s

The cowboys are dying; fenceposts
And wires and steel chains and ghosts;
The wind sweeps what it wants
Across the prairies, taunts

The wheat-blown fields, yellowed
With fall. It is ending, now,
The age of the cowboy, when men
Were alone with themselves, ten

At a time, the open air of the New
World closing; when migrant boys
Looked west in leather hats, their slang

Pierced with Polish accents, city noise.
But we've reached California and
The cowboys are sinking into the sea,

Each looking at the other with a wild
Surmise—still searching for
Whatever it is that makes men free.

Poem For Andrew Jackson

Yes, you are an asshole
But so are we: there
Is only so much you can take
And take and take without
Losing whatever it was
You at first sought to feed.

There is a story of you on
The battlefield: a newborn
Son laying in the hands
Of his dead Creek parents
Before you adopted him.
He died later, at seventeen.

There is another story of you
Just before your inauguration:
Your wife dead and you taking
Strength from believing
Politics had stolen her
From you. *A broken
Heart*, you declared,
Is what killed her.

And so it went: your life a
Circle of taking and being
Taken from, and yet remaining
Hungry, as we are now,
No matter what it was
You at first sought to feed.

On Comparing Post-Sleep Disorientation (Also Known As "Confusional Arousal") To Fievel Discovering America And Being Surprised By What He Sees

there is a waking
moment
where all is not

lost nor is it beheld
like the swift bleaching
away of a sheet

but that diminishes
slightly
with each breath

so too in life and travel
mouse
where harbors and towns

fight mental mismatch
now that you sift
alone in this

world the factories
clank like tired clocks
where

here is nothing
like you were just
imagining it to be

On Thinking About Nazism, Walt Disney Late At Night

After Larkin

Going back to bed after a piss
I lift the heavy sheets and slip
Into bed and am startled by

The light, wandering in through
A crack in the curtains.
True, it is laughable:

The way routine draws us back
To the same spot every night
To sleep, or the way the clouds part

Outside as if in reverence to a light
That's not their own. True, one shivers
At the prospect of starting from scratch.

But so too does one shiver after a 3 a.m.
Piss at the thought of being alone.
O light! O dawn that's never ending!

History arcs like urine bent by gravity
And rots like rained-on trash, lucky never
To hope of starting over again.

Mouse Discovers The Existence Of Evil

Porchlight tumbler and charred leaves:
The wind takes what it wants away
Dancing through the autumn darkness.

The hierarchy of the yard outside:
One thing eats another eats another
As if each were created just to survive.

But even that hierarchy breaks: as when
Suddenly awakened to a pain that could
Not be more real, or violent, or complete.

Advice For A Teenage Mouse

> *You who do not know how the mind is joined*
> *to the body know nothing of the works of God.*
> —Ecclesiastes

I.

They will tell you on a clear
Day there is one thing
Between the earth and stars.
Do not ask them what it is.
Consider whether you care
Enough to ask yourself.

II.

> *America goes on, goes on*
> *Laughing, and Harding was a fool.*
> —James Wright

They will speak in absolutes
Because it is easier that way
Making gods out of presidents
And then shaming them. Do not be
Embarrassed. There is a saying
That says that he who says nothing
Is afraid of saying everything.
Speak out loud but do not
Be afraid. Let judgment come
Like ten thousand sheets of rain
Dropped by clouds that drift
Without purpose, even as they
Separate the earth from its stars.

Mouse Tries To Feel Good About The Future

How could each day not be
Better than the last! For I am
Starving here and in America
There are so many clothes.

No, the clouds will break
And the sunlight is sure to be
Let in and if not, it must
At least a little, at some
Point soon.

Before Dawn

Here, in the
Early morning,

Where darkness
Fades like red

Wine stains—
Somehow gradually,

Somehow not
At all—if only

Love for something
Growing older

Could render it
New again.

Poem About A Lost Hat

In the water that surged
With last night's storm
All things are floating
Down the Mississippi:
Charcoal wet with
Mud; felt patches
Once affixed to cheap
Couches; drank cans
Of beer.

And then there
Is this, almost ten feet
Out: a tiny mouse stuck
In an old hat, drifting
On its back, his circular
Belly pointed upwards
At the sky.

How he must
Be hungry! But also how
He must not see, from his
Vantage, that there is food
In the debris, drifting all
Around; that the river
Takes both the good and
The bad, indiscriminately.

Mouse's Prayer

After Claudel

Once again, Lord, the currents of the sea take me with them. Each is yours and not one is new. When I die, let nothing make me suffer. Bury me between my father and my mother in a bed of grass and let nothing make me suffer. Let the sacrament of my body dissolve into the linen earth and my heart pound itself softly to rest. As did Abraham, as did Isaac, as did Jacob: so let me. Now, the streets wander towards the countryside in lost desolation, lapping backwards into themselves. They are a poem without form because they are words and there is no form in them. My eyes are heavy and the sky is mist and the space is as silent as water every time I look. Let me stop looking, Lord, as long as I am here. The days rise. I cannot ask anymore. Let the currents carry me, Lord, let them whisper to me where we are going. Let them awaken me to a river that tells me we are going home.

Mouse Doubts Poetry's Utility

I want to create
You said, the silence everywhere,
I want to make
Something that lives
Even after, you
Said, I die.

But, I said,
Your things don't know,
I said, the quiet now pronounced,
Not even themselves starting
The moment
They're made.

Instructions For What To Do Upon Losing Your Family

On Reuniting With Loved Ones

Somewhere a leaf
Tinkers with the grass
At the edge of a forest.

That leaf is fallen, and
Will not stay.

      For close by,
The high-up trees are
Bending

      And the wind
Is sure to have its way.

Haircut

(As Told to a 3-Year-Old Going to a Barber for the First Time)

Nothing's worth losing
You're ready for

So jump up on that seat
And be bibbed

And do not fight your crying
As each hair hits the floor.

Bath

After Merrill

The faucet thrusts
Its water   towards
The tub   like
The beginning
          And the end:
Dropped from on high
A disoriented   thud
The bathwater rising
Up   and   up,
Circling the plug.

Mouse Makes Love

After Pessoa

Sleep, enchanted, while I watch…
Breathe softly so that I may dream…
I am not happy.
I want you as in a dream
So there is something left to wake to.

Your breathing hides my cold
Desire like this ruffled blanket.
My cravings are wearinesses.
I'll never give them to you.

Sleep, enchanted, sleep…
I've dreamt you so carefully
That dreaming is enchantment
So long as my eyes are closed.

Mouse Breaks Up With Girlfriend

After Rilke

Your body trembles: mine will be rich for you.
Often, you weren't as poor: I will pardon you
For forgetting me.
When watching you leave
Let me remind you nothing on its own is true.

Granted, we are not alone, but together a solitary two:
One and the other.
How much we take and is owed the other
No one imagines.
And still, nothing is asked. One learns from our silences:
However much they hurt.

**Father Mouse Loses His Temper And
Yells At A 3-Year-Old During A Birthday Party**

Life is EXACTLY like the spaghetti
YOU ordered with butter and salt
That came with NONE of those things.
It is not that YOU cannot control it.
NONE of us can. Instead, EVEN IF
The tomato sauce you did NOT WANT
And did NOT EXPECT is soaked
With ROT there is NOTHING
But what you HAVE BEEN given and
That is ALL THERE IS left to eat.

**Father Mouse Apologizes By Attempting
To Explain The Meaning Of Life**

everything is new here
because each moment is forbidden
from repeating the last
therefore celebrate every second
even if time is relentless in its
passing does not give you
what you want no matter
how much you wanted it
instead know that each one
of us is here together
however long this lasts

Advice For A Grown-Up Mouse

After Pessoa

Build a fence around who you dream
You are. Then, in the most visible holes
In the grating, place what you are most
Proud of. Place pictures, place reams
Of orchids, for they are exotic. Drape
These achievements in the periphery.

Let them hide the emptinesses which host
In the center, where you have planted nothing.
Let each who passes your fence believe
That it was tailored for them the most.
But where you are yours let the growing
To itself, and know that gardens naturally

Do not overgrow, are rather dust to sieve
Unattended. Here, between this center,
Divide yourself twofold and let this suffice.
One who knows nothing but his fence
And another who dreams his solitary core,
Knows the chord of his praying rings empty
With dust. Not fire. Not water. Not ice.

Dialogue Between Father And Son, In Two Parts

Keep walking… for it is raining.
Do not be afraid… it is only cold.

When you were sick
At night the doors opened in the wind.

When you were sick at night
The doors closed as if they were dancing.

When you were sick of hearing
The house moved in the ruffled wind I left.

I left the tired house alone,
When your sickness sickened you.

*

If I was there, I would not have left.
If I was there, I would tell you

Your sickness is your life
For even now, it is not ready for the end it reaps.

I would tell you to keep walking
As if that's what you were meant for.

Your story has not ended,
Even if no one is there to watch.

Four Endings For A Cartoon Mouse

I.

A tack-on, really, to the real story:
From Shostka, Russia, to the port
Of New Orleans to a train car
Limping westward, each arrival
Better than the last.

II.

But now the end has come; there
Will be no more arrivals; and this
Desert was not meant to be your
Home. Here: Nevada burnt lust
And never-ending sand, where
You will be forgotten like all this
Dust: created but then dispersed.

III.

You grew illusions like lilacs pinned
To a tree, tired perhaps of moving, but
Also, I'd imagine, eager for other things.

IV.

O travelers of worn soles and frayed
Pictures and yellowed frames! Each
One of you a muted flower
That dreamt a wilderness
But then resolved to fall, and wait,
And blossom, as if in progress, when
Really there was no progress at all.

Author's Note

The poems in this book are based on the story of Fievel Mousekewitz, as depicted in the cartoon movies *Fievel: An American Tail* (1986) and *An American Tail: Fievel Goes West* (1991). In the movies, the Mousekewitz family emigrates from Russia to America in the late 1800s after a pogrom in their hometown of Shostka. Early on in their journey, a young Fievel is separated from his family and forced to contend with the harsh reality of America and its violent and rapacious cats. The same themes dominate the second movie, but this time with the Mousekewitz family seeking freedom and opportunity as they leave New York City for the Wild West. In each movie, Fievel is reunited with his family only after embarking on dangerous and harrowing adventures.

The poems in this book were written over a period of 15 years, beginning, approximately, in 2006.

"Immigrant Mouse Arrives In New York, Circa 1900" was inspired by Federico García Lorca's "Oda A Walt Whitman."

"Old Clock" was inspired by a small grandfather clock maintained by my great-grandfather, Philip Amsterdam, which he passed on to his youngest daughter, my great-aunt, Jean Foreman.

"On Thinking About Nazism, Walt Disney Late At Night" was inspired by Philip Larkin's "Sad Steps."

"Advice For A Teenage Mouse" contains a quote attributed to the Book of Ecclesiastes, which French essayist and philosopher Michel de Montaigne is said to have written as an inscription on his ceiling, as detailed in Saul Frampton's "When I Am Playing With My Cat, How Do I Know She Is Not Playing With Me?" The quote attributed to James Wright is from "Two Poems about President Harding."

"Mouse's Prayer" was inspired by Paul Claudel's "Dissolution."

"Bath" was inspired by James Merrill's "A Downward Look."

Mouse Breaks Up With Girlfriend was inspired by Rainer Maria Rilke's "Brother body is poor."

"Instructions For What To Do Upon Losing Your Family: Write A Will" was originally entitled "Instructions To My Wife For After I Am Gone."

About the Author

Andrew Burt lives in Washington, DC, with his wife and two sons. This is his first book of poetry.

The Jewish Poetry Project

jpoetry.us

Ben Yehuda Press

From the Coffee House of Jewish Dreamers: Poems of Wonder and Wandering and the Weekly Torah Portion by Isidore Century

"Isidore Century is a wonderful poet. His poems are funny, deeply observed, without pretension." – *The Jewish Week*

The House at the Center of the World: Poetic Midrash on Sacred Space by Abe Mezrich

"Direct and accessible, Mezrich's midrashic poems often tease profound meaning out of his chosen Torah texts. These poems remind us that our Creator is forgiving, that the spiritual and physical can inform one another, and that the supernatural can be carried into the everyday."
—Yehoshua November, author of *God's Optimism*

we who desire: Poems and Torah riffs by Sue Swartz

"Sue Swartz does magnificent acrobatics with the Torah. She takes the English that's become staid and boring, and adds something that's new and strange and exciting. These are poems that leave a taste in your mouth, and you walk away from them thinking, what did I just read? Oh, yeah. It's the Bible."
—Matthue Roth, author of *Yom Kippur A Go-Go*

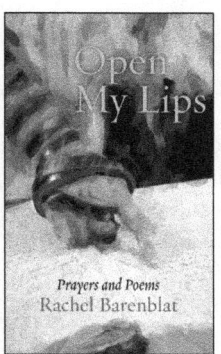

Open My Lips: Prayers and Poems by Rachel Barenblat

"Barenblat's God is a personal God—one who lets her cry on His shoulder, and who rocks her like a colicky baby. These poems bridge the gap between the ineffable and the human. This collection will bring comfort to those with a religion of their own, as well as those seeking a relationship with some kind of higher power."
—Satya Robyn, author of *The Most Beautiful Thing*

Words for Blessing the World: Poems in Hebrew and English by Herbert J. Levine

"These writings express a profoundly earth-based theology in a language that is clear and comprehensible. These are works to study and learn from."
—Rodger Kamenetz, author of *The Jew in the Lotus*

Shiva Moon: Poems by Maxine Silverman

"The poems, deeply felt, are spare, spoken in a quiet but compelling voice, as if we were listening in to her inner life. This book is a precious record of the transformation saying Kaddish can bring."
—Howard Schwartz, author of *The Library of Dreams*

is: heretical Jewish blessings and poems by Yaakov Moshe (Jay Michaelson)

"Finally, Torah that speaks to and through the lives we are actually living: expanding the tent of holiness to embrace what has been cast out, elevating what has been kept down, advancing what has been held back, reveling in questions, revealing contradictions."
—Eden Pearlstein, aka eprhyme

Texts to the Holy: Poems
by Rachel Barenblat

"These poems are remarkable, radiating a love of God that is full bodied, innocent, raw, pulsating, hot, drunk. I can hardly fathom their faith but am grateful for the vistas they open. I will sit with them, and invite you to do the same."
—Merle Feld, author of *A Spiritual Life*

The Sabbath Bee: Love Songs to Shabbat
by Wilhelmina Gottschalk

"Torah, say our sages, has seventy faces. As these prose poems reveal, so too does Shabbat. Here we meet Shabbat as familiar housemate, as the child whose presence transforms a family, as a spreading tree, as an annoying friend who insists on being celebrated, as a woman, as a man, as a bee, as the ocean."
—Rachel Barenblat, author of *The Velveteen Rabbi's Haggadah*

All the Holes Line Up: Poems and Translations
by Zackary Sholem Berger

"Spare and precise, Berger's poems gaze unflinchingly at—but also celebrate—human imperfection in its many forms. And what a delight that Berger also includes in this collection a handful of his resonant translations of some of the great Yiddish poets." —Yehoshua November, author of *God's Optimism* and *Two World Exist*

How to Bless the New Moon:
Songs of the Sovereign and the Icon
by Rachel Kann

"Rachel Kann is a master wordsmith. Her poems are rich in content, packed with life's wisdom and imbued with soul. May this collection of her work enable more of the world to enjoy her offerings."
—Sarah Yehudit Schneider, author of *You Are What You Hate* and *Kabbalistic Writings on the Nature of Masculine and Feminine*

Into My Garden
by David Caplan

"The beauty of Caplan's book is that it is not polemical. It does not set out to win an argument or ask you whether you've put your tefillin on today. These gentle poems invite the reader into one person's profound, ambiguous religious experience."
—*The Jewish Review of Books*

Between the Mountain and the Land is the Lesson: Poetic Midrash on Sacred Community
by Abe Mezrich

"Abe Mezrich cuts straight back to the roots of the Midrashic tradition, sermonizing as a poet, rather than idealogue. Best of all, Abe knows how to ask questions and avoid the obvious answers."
—Jake Marmer, author of *Jazz Talmud*

NOKADDISH: Poems in the Void
by Hanoch Guy Kaner

"A subversive, midrashic play with meanings—specifically Jewish meanings, and then the reversal and negation of these meanings."
—Robert G. Margolis

An Added Soul: Poems for a New Old Religion
by Herbert J. Levine

"These poems are remarkable, radiating a love of God that is full bodied, innocent, raw, pulsating, hot, drunk. I can hardly fathom their faith but am grateful for the vistas they open. I will sit with them, and invite you to do the same."
—Merle Feld, author of *A Spiritual Life*.

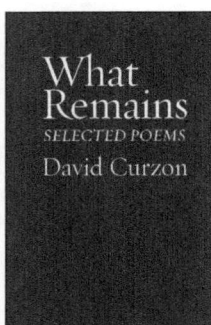

What Remains
by David Curzon

"Aphoristic, ekphrastic, and precise revelations animate WHAT REMAINS. In his stunning rewriting of Psalm 1 and other biblical passages, Curzon shows himself to be a fabricator, a collector, and an heir to the literature, arts, and wisdom traditions of the planet."
—Alicia Ostriker, author of *The Volcano and After*

The Shortest Skirt in Shul
by Sass Oron

"These poems exuberantly explore gender, Torah, the masks we wear, and the way our bodies (and the ways we wear them) at once threaten stable narratives, and offer the kind of liberation that saves our lives."
—Alicia Jo Rabins, author of *Divinity School*, composer of *Girls In Trouble*

Walking Triptychs
by Ilya Gutner

These are poems from when I walked about Shanghai and thought about the meaning of the Holocaust.

Book of Failed Salvation
by Julia Knobloch

"These beautiful poems express a tender longing for spiritual, physical, and emotional connection. They detail a life in movement—across distances, faith, love, and doubt."
—David Caplan, author of *Into My Garden*

Daily Blessings: Poems on Tractate Berakhot
by Hillel Broder

"Hillel Broder does not just write poetry about the Talmud; he also draws out the Talmud's poetry, finding lyricism amidst legality and re-setting the Talmud's rich images like precious gems in end-stopped lines of verse."
—Ilana Kurshan, author of *If All the Seas Were Ink*

The Missing Jew: Poems 1976-2022
by Rodger Kamenetz

"How does Rodger Kamenetz manage to have so singular a voice and at the same time precisely encapsulate the world view of an entire generation (also mine) of text-hungry American Jews born in the middle of the twentieth century?"
—Jacqueline Osherow, author of *Ultimatum from Paradise* and *My Lookalike at the Krishna Temple: Poems*

The Red Door: A dark fairy tale told in poems
by Shawn C. Harris

"THE RED DOOR, like its poet author Shawn C. Harris, transcends genres and identities. It is an exploration in crossing worlds. It brings together poetry and story telling, imagery and life events, spirit and body, the real and the fantastic, Jewish past and Jewish present, to spin one tale."
—Einat Wilf, author of *The War of Return*

The Matter of Families
by Robert H. Deluty

"Robert Deluty's career-spanning collection of New and Selected poems captures the essence of his work: the power of love, joy, and connection, all tied together with the poet's glorious sense of humor. This book is Deluty's masterpiece."
—Richard M. Berlin, M.D., author of *Freud on My Couch*

The Five Books of Limericks
by Rhonda Rosenheck

"A biblical commentary that is truly unique. Each chapter of the Torah is distilled into its own limerick, leading the reader to reconsider the meaning of the original text, and opening avenues for interpretation that are both fun and insightful."
—Rabbi Hillel Norry

Bits and Pieces
by Edward Pomerantz

"A stunning tapestry of family life in the 40s and 50s. Like all great poetry, Pomerantz's work expands after reading. Each poem is exquisitely structured, often with a stunning ending, into a masterful whole."
—Alan Ziegler, editor of SHORT: An International Anthology

Words for a Dazzling Firmament: Poems/Readings on Bereishit Through Shemot
by Abe Mezrich

"Mezrich is a cultivated craftsman— interpretively astute, sonically deliberate, and spiritually cunning."
—Zohar Atkins, author of Nineveh

Everything Thaws
by R. B. Lemberg

"Full of glacier-sharp truths, and moments revealed between words like bodies beneath melting permafrost. As it becomes increasingly plain how deeply our world is shaped by war and climate change and grief and anger, articulating that shape feels urgent and necessary and painful and healing."
—Ruthanna Emrys, author of A Half-Built Garden

Ode to the Dove
An illustrated, bilingual edition of a Yiddish poem by Abraham Sutzkever
Zackary Sholem Berger, translator
Liora Ostroff, Illustrator

"An elegant volume for lovers of poetry."
—Justin Cammy, translator of Sutzkever, *From the Vilna Ghetto to Nuremberg: Memoir and Testimony*

Poems for a Cartoon Mouse
by Andrew Burt

"Andrew Burt's poetry magnifies the vanishingly small line between danger and safety. This collection asks whether order is an illusion that veils chaos, or vice-versa, juxtaposing images from the Bible with animated films."
—Ari Shapiro, host of NPR's *All Things Considered*

Old Shul
by Pinny Bulman

"Nostalgia gives way to a tender theology, a softly chuckling illumination from within the heart of/as a beautiful, broken sanctuary, somehow both gritty and fragile, grimy and iridescent – not unlike faith itself."
—Jake Marmer, author of *Cosmic Diaspora*

Feet In L.A., But My Womb Lives In Jerusalem, My Breath In Vermont
by Lori Levy

"Reading through Lori Levy's new book of poems takes my breath away. With no pretense whatsoever, they leap, alive, from the page until this reader felt as if she were living Levy's life. How does the author do it?"
—Mary Jo Balistreri, author of *Still*

www.ingramcontent.com/pod-product-compliance
Lightning Source LLC
LaVergne TN
LVHW041346080426
835512LV00006B/642